Soul Sister Sonnets and Images

by

William Stephen Bowden

authorHOUSE™

1663 LIBERTY DRIVE, SUITE 200
BLOOMINGTON, INDIANA 47403
(800) 839-8640
WWW.AUTHORHOUSE.COM

First published by AuthorHouse 06/17/05

ISBN: 1-4208-3076-7 (e)
ISBN: 1-4208-3077-5 (sc)

Printed in the United States of America
Bloomington, Indiana

This book is printed on acid-free paper.

I conjured a soliloquy, all about the sister, and I dressed it all up in a sonnet. It is a sonnet consisting of all the instruments of her existence and I stamped her personal essence on it.

I created a trilogy inside of a sonnet, and I did it with truth telling conviction, in it I documented her very being in clear and non-fiction diction! Unrehearsed but in composite verse, with painstaking thought, I eagerly sought to chronicle her amazing worth and to narrate accurately her-story first.

Thus I composed a symphonic sonnet, true to the original receiver graphically passed from she to me, the living believer, a soul sister's story, in all of its glory, captured complete in a sonnet, I lived it, I loved it, and passionately I wrote it, and I etched my personal signature on it!

The Sonneteer

Dedicated to Mena, who instilled in me the
Inspiration to write. Thank you momma for your
Brilliant insight...

FOREWORD

Not many people understand poetry as a valid art form of personal expression. Poetry is a truly wonderful way to share a personal gift. I have known William for close to thirty years, and was highly flattered when he asked for my honest reaction to this work. William watched me grow from a young girl wanting to express her art and not believing in herself, to a confident woman who did and received a degree from the fashion institute of technology along the way. Thank you William for being a mentor and a friend.

As you read the forth coming pages, you will understand how personal William's thoughts are on women. Women of all dimensions. He has a unique vision which started some twenty plus years ago and culminates in his passion for writing and having his message heard. William is a deep thinker and not prone to revealing his true self to the outside world.

A reserved man, he studies, he thinks, and the pages of this book explode into words, and such a play with words does he exhibit! Men might not understand why he writes that he does. "why would he write the truth about how I think?" "I shouldn't tell my wife, my woman, or my significant other how I really feel". Women on the other hand, will read these lines see themselves and wish the words were written for them. The age old questions women have long asked are answered between the covers of this book. William Stephen Bowden I salute you for a job well done.

Peace

Toni R. Todd
The Doll Artisan

Social worker
Textiles production management
Consultant

FACES LIKE OURS

Faces like ours are impressive to view, they are reflective of every tone, and every hue. Our faces come in grapefruit beige and charcoal sage, and purples darker than blue. Our faces are sandy and tanned, bronzed and browned, licorice and lily white down.

Faces like ours are new and old, our faces have features both soft and bold. Our faces are smooth our faces are creased, our complexions are ruddy, our complexions are bleached.

Faces like ours stand out in a crowd, faces like ours send a message out loud. Our face is god's window to you, most of us have only one face,. Some others have two. Whether your face is dirty or clean, whether your face is pleasant or mean, your face may be lighter, your face may be blacker, your face may be whiter it really makes no difference what your complexion is: because in god's eyes all faces like ours look exactly like his.

SOUL SISTERS IN THE PLANET

What makes a soul sister in the planet? What ever it is that does, how do we explain it? How would she who is without soul, seek to attain it? What is the common denominator which makes soul sisters kin, is it the complexion or the texture of their skin, or could it be some cultural characteristic rooted from deep within?

Is a soul sister in this planet of any persusion other than pure caucasion? Must her racial identity necessarily show for everyone to know? Is she simply a female of color from American society of every shade and every variety, is she of southern extract, or is she an urban bred project Deb to be exact, or perhaps she is just any dark skinned, brown, or yellow girl from any and all regions of this world, maybe a soul sister in this planet is just a warm blooded universal matriarcal phenomena encompassing the entire feminine gammit.

How much soul glows in a warm nosed Eskimoe or a painted toed Ebo? I don't know, what about a Nubian, a Peruvian, an Argentine or an Aboriginine? Can the soul in them be seen? Are soul sisters equally dispersed prominately around this earth? Are they intrinsically related by their particular milieu? I ask you! What is an Indian? Is an Aztec different from an Inca, and are they distantly related to a Mandinka? Are they soul sisters too? If so, what about Iranians, Jordanians and Albanians, if so, what about dark Jews?

To all sisters around the globe, skin white as snow, bronzed, or yellow gold, to the blackest charcoal, to you I ask, face unmasked are you a soul sister in this planet too? If so, I write these selective sonnets especially for you!

SHE IS!

She is
Fairest among tens of thousands as she reigns
Sovereign and serene

She is
As calming as the Rock of Gibraltar steadfast
Amidst a sea of chaos

She is

A beacon!   A visionary!

An inspiration!

A GOOD MAN'S KIND OF WOMAN

A good man's kind of woman is, exclusively and undeniably his. She is always there, totally committed to their mutual affairs. She loves and appreciates her good man for himself first, and she is not overly concerned with his liniage, or his kinage, or his monetary worth. She is the kind of woman who is comfortable and confident on her own two feet, she is the kind of woman whom all good men seek to meet.

A good man's kind of woman is not overbearing, she is the non-comparing, always sharing kind who makes up her own mind. She is the kind of woman with whom a good man can relate to well, she understands his emotions, he can share his inner secrets with her and she will never ever tell. She knows the kind of man he wants to be, she reads his heart but never his mind. If something seems wrong, she is not to shy to ask him why, and she is not afraid of what she may find.

A good man's kind of woman can draw her man to her and yet still give him his space, he can take her to any place of good taste, and she doesn't require a lot of makeup to put her face in place. She is a natural beauty, a vision of charm clutched to his arm, she always looks trim and fit, it's inherent in the way she moves in how she stands and sits. She is as relaxed in heels and a shimmering gown with a sable stole wrapped all around as she is in a skirt or slacks or blue jeans and one of her good man's oversized shirts. Some how for a good man's kind of woman it all seems to work.

A good man's kind of women must, be the kind of woman whom he can completely trust. She is even tempered and pro-active but not excessively re-active. She is assertively expressive but not dominating and possessive. A good man's kind of woman refuses to fight, she prefers settling differences over dinner by candle light if necessary deep into the night. They may stroll together arm in arm in fair or inclement weather or dance the night away together soothingly cradled to her good man's chest and to his caress light like a feather, maybe the difficulties become better.

Because a good man's kind of woman is his sterling clean domestic queen, his chosen spouse, the keeper of his house. By his side with a smile she will walk with him down the aisle to become his bride. A mature lady, his very special girl, a modern woman of the world, she is his heavenly dream in an earthly female human being. A good man's kind of woman!

WHEN OUR EYES FINALLY MEET

When our eyes finally meet, they will show no deceit, our egos and super egos will not have to compete. There will be no spontaneous profilific impressions, only positive expressions. When our eyes finally meet, they will remain firmly afixed, they will never turn askance into some fleeting glance. Our admiring gaze toward each other will not stray, it will stay. Our heads will not bow, turn, or look away.

When our eyes finally meet, our eyes will also speak, smiles will be prepared and displayed with intricate care, and features will be featured, beauty beheld trust will prevail and joy will be victorious and the personal stimulation will be glorious.

When our eyes finally meet, there will be no raised brows, no batting or blinking, no cause for negative thinking, our eyes will light up. The only tears will be tears of joy and the only fear will be mine, lest your eyes not see into my heart or hear my song and the love that I will bring, when our eyes finally, finally, finally, meet.

A FLOWER IN HER HAIR

There is no more a fascinating lady fair, then that fair lady who will boldly dare to wear a soft pretty flower in her hair. That tantalizing temptress with that certain ilk, mysterious eyes, sensuous lips and black or flaxon hair, smooth like spun silk, she is a wild flower in her own right, she is that firy siren who can shine brightly through the darkest midnight.

She is Gypsy Rose Lee, Marilyn Monroe, and Carmen Jones. She is Josephine Baker, Maria Callus, and Evita Peron. She is tennis sisters, Venus and Serena, Cher, Madonna, and Queen Wilhelmina. Just as Billie Holiday was lady day, "Billie with a lily on her ear". Bette Midler is the rose, the divine Mz. M, a show woman first, with no peer, and no fear.

These original divas, these flamboyant vamps, never have to display their rear, never have to strip almost bare, they simply demand and command your attention span, sometimes with a flower in their hair.

PROJECTS GIRL

This projects girl don't have no tight behind. This projects girl is the most adaptable and versatile girl you will ever find. She is equally at ease in work school or play, this projects girl is a lady first in every way. She has her own inimible urban style and a very distinctive and confident smile. That lingers in your mind's eye for a very very long long while.

When situations dictate, she can be tough enough, but not so tough that her femininity will suffer much. She won't complain, or stand and pout when the service on both elevators just happen to go out. She will climb fifteen flights of cold cement steps and broken ceiling lights, and return later dressed like royalty going out that night.

This projects girl is sidewalk and playground bred, braided pigtails, ribbons, and barretts adorned her head. She can jump double dutch wearing tight blue jeans with a small purse tightly in her clutch. She goes to church on Sunday, but she ain't no church girl for you to see, an avid connoisseur of the world current events is she.

This projects girl is going to travel far, she's going to compete well and she is going to excell. She knows how far she can possibly go, because of former project girls like Diana Ross, Jackie Joyner, and the revered Flo-Jo. This projects girl knows well that where she is going and what she will ultimately find, is as wide ranging and expandsive as the creativity of her own mind. So like fine wine, just give this projects girl her own space and her own time, and this city flower will blossom sweetly and the girl from the housing projects will turn out just fine.

THAT WOMAN WEARING THAT HAT

I love that women who is wearing that hat, that confident woman who knows where her head is at. That woman who is wearing that stunningly beautiful blue bonnet with the pretty flowers adorned on it, complete with colorful ribbons and bows, that classy woman wearing that classy hat knows, exactly what her headwear shows.

It shows that regardless of where she goes, she is conscious and proud of her unique hats and her trend setting clothes. Whether young or old, she is definately independent, original, and bold. Her statement is right there in her headdress whenever she steps out there amongst the world's best dressed, from the top of her head down, she easily rises far above the best around.

Just observe how squarely her hat sits as she sits, knowing that for her it is the perfect style and the perfect fit. On mother's day, on woman's day, on Easter Sunday it is of her that I am amazed, it is on her that I fix my gaze, it is of her that I must confess, for me that woman in that hat is the absolute best!

AN AMERICAN WOMAN OF POWER

An American woman of power is the type of woman whom some men abhor, they abhor her because they don't know how to adore her and can't place themselves before her, because she's too independent, too resourceful and resplendent, and of herself she's so sure.

She is straight forward and direct, a go getter who demands respect self taught and can't be bought, she has an overide of pride and talent on her side, she loves to lead and hates to concede, when a crisis arises, there are no surprises in the way she responds with all necessary speed. In times of crisis, she is the one we need.

This woman of power is no practical joker, she is just an effective and persuasive peace broker. No hotshot, just our best shot. When the chips are down, she is simply the best around. She is not a jetsetter, but is a definate trendsetter. As a mediator, negotiator, and educator, there are few better, an elegant public speaker, she is often mentioned as a potential high office seeker. Politically she's an independent advocate and a bi-partisan moderate. Protocol doesn't scare her at all, she doesn't always heed. But she is infinately qualified with the ability to lead. Well bred and well read, she is solidly focused with a level head.

An American woman of power also keeps an orderly house and out of necessity she has a tolerant and understanding spouse. Her children are well schooled, but never pampered or ruled. She capably mothers them but never smothers them, she is all of our precious gem, our woman of the hour, this dynamic American woman of power.

DAZZLE

She is upper crust, bred from class, she was a debutante girl, she is society's wonderful gift to the world. In season she wears sable and fine silk and female fashions with a New York or Paris label, designer dresses and gowns of the most exclusive ilk. Her elegance is real, it is factual, she is an actual emperoress, not just another fairy tale princess of fable, she is a diva. She is a true first lady and the whole wide world is her table.

She is the ambassadress of charm, comfortable in the company of kings and presidents, and prime ministers in arm. Her voice and diction is clear but soft, smooth like velour with just a hint of amour, not suggestive or outwardly seductive, just calm and confident and assertively sure. Her aura preceeds her as she enters a room and captures a place, the anticipation is stifling until you finally see her delicate porcelain like face.

There is a dancing dimple on each soft cheek, and her hazel green eyes are just filled with her own unique mytique. Her golden crowned hair is always combed and coiffed naturally in place, perfectly and tastefully styled down to the very last trace. First impressions are often deceiving, but being in her presence means instantly believing. She is America's brand new day's surprise arrising with each sunrise, our true queen of the ball, dazzling before our very eyes, she is simply the fairest lady of them all.

THE REVERAND SISTER LOVE

Who is it, who is changing the gender and the face of grace? Who is delivering the word in a way in which it has never before been heard? Who is on an anointing mission with a far far reaching vision? Nominational or non, ordained or beyond, it is the right reverand sister love whom I write of.

Whether robed and collared, or striking in a smart suit with stunning hat crowning, her ministry is astounding. From the pulpit she stands as tall as anyone as her congregation sits. For hers is a congregation equalate female to male, uncompromised non-politicized and certainly not for sale! It is a ministry which nurtures its youth in truth, which guides its adolescents and comforts its convelescents, the reverand sister love feeds the hungry and shelters the homeless, she will pray for the sick and visit the lonely, and the right reverand sister love refuses to minister to one group or one class only.

It is truly a special kind of person who is a lady and a pastor, a person who is answering the master's call and at the same time destructing the "male preachers only wall", while still being a mother like few others, feeding her family and leading her church while still not hiding or abiding on some lofty perch. Her church is one church! God's church! Which seeks to feed every heart and to fill every head, and to assure that every spiritual appetite will be fed.

The reverand sister love will be anyone's spiritual guide. She will pray with you, she will stay with you, she will baptise and eulogize for hers is the full universal ministry centered in love and honesty and free of sinistry, with pride I write of the reverand sister love in whom you can confide.

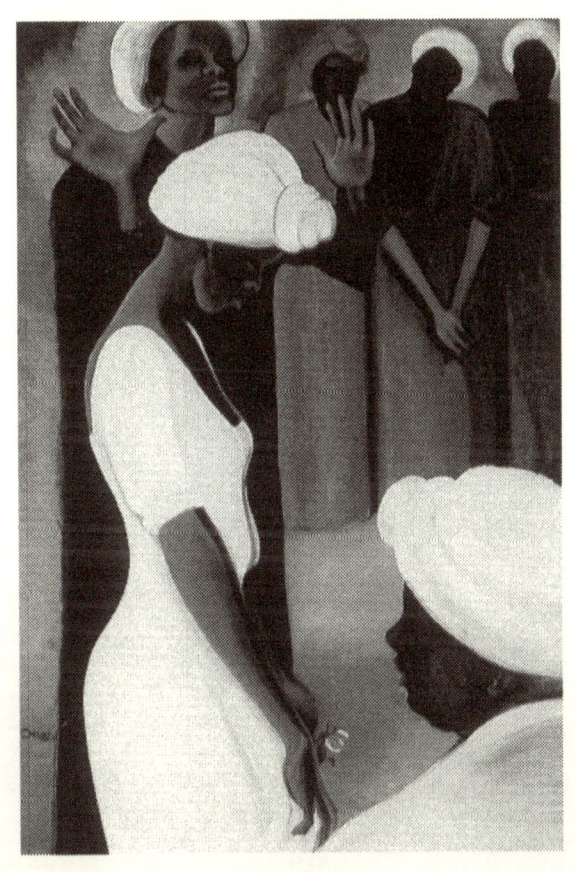

THE INIMITABLE CHIOR GIRLS

The inimitable choir girls always pray first, and then the inimitable choir girls begin to rehearse, during which time they catch up on all the church news, and air their views, the entire evening long, until it gets late, and then after substantial debate, the inimitable choir girls agree on the Sunday morning songs.

A half hour before service, the inimitable choir girls prepare, they are primping and powdering, and touching up their hair. They loosen their bra straps and pull up their slips, they lotion down their legs, and moisten their lips. Then the inimitable choir girls join their hands in prayer, and leave all of their negative issues in that choir room right there.

While singing the opening hymn, the inimitable choir girls in their grandeur file, triumphantly up the sanctuary aisle, straight up into the choir loft where immediately any lingering concerns are routinely dropped off.

The inimitable choir girls are in magnificent voice on this beautiful Sunday morn, and they look impeccable with their new hair styles and beautiful smiles adorned and their freshly pressed and cleaned choir robes being worn. The soloists sing so sweetly that they fill everyone's soul completely, higher and higher their songs take the church people, their voices soaring far and above the church steeple, now they are vigorously stomping and clapping, faster and faster, encouraging the pastor and giving all praises due to the almighty master. By no means are these some ordinary church girls, no sir, these are virtual gospel pearls, these are the original inimitable choir girls!

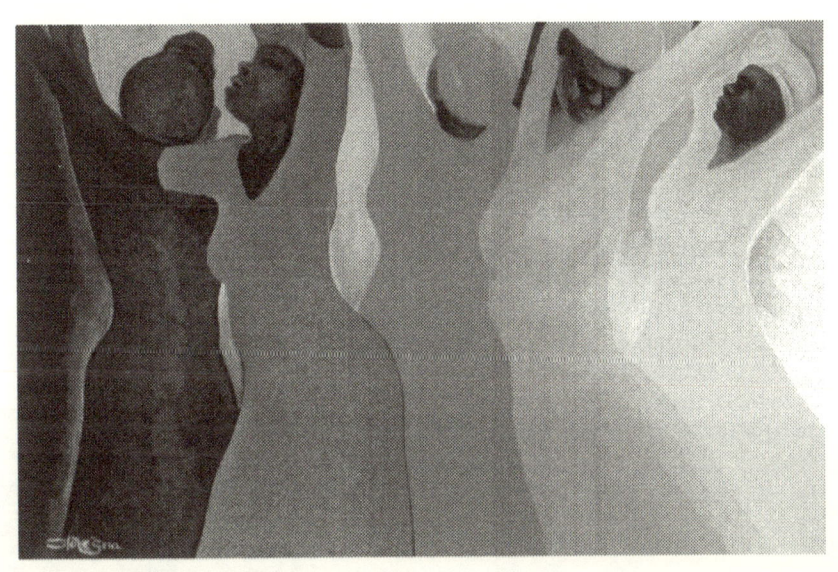

A MAN'S IMAGE OF BEAUTIFUL

A man's image of beautiful need not always refer to prettiness or sex, ultimately it is a woman's essence which truly rules. The image that a beautiful woman leaves must be able to be totally believed. It is of a lovely romantic, an organic lady natural proud and unafraid to wear her hair in locks and braids and even bald, still remaining stately and tall.

A man's image of beautiful is of dark opal almond eyes and synchronized chocolate vanilla thighs, shimmering and strutting. It is of a body fragrance so feminine and clean that it can almost be felt or visually seen. Angelically soft skin so smooth that even when gold or platinum clad or accentually bejeweled it is able to glow on its own.

A man's image of beautiful is finger tips that can be tasted like warm butter through their touch, and honey breath tongues and fruity lips that talk through kisses bringing an undeniable message. It is of that haunting smile which lingers in a man's mind eye after the woman is long out of sight. It is the scent of sweet feet bathed in oil and crowned with pearl anklets which seem to barely ever alight, a beautiful sight.

A man's image of beautiful is a woman who illicits elation in him. They are a match, a pair that looks good together, perfect partners for dining, for strolling, for dancing in sync as if they are physically linked. When a man's image of beautiful becomes reality, he says finally, finally, finally.

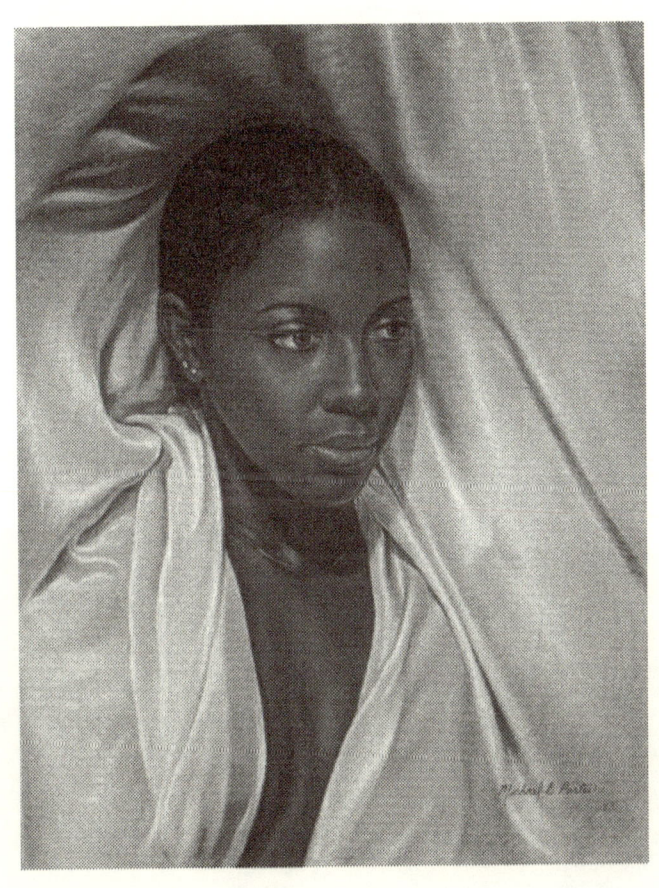

BROWN COFFEE

How do I like my morning coffee? I like mine like you! Dark, deep, and delicious, with just a skance of milk or cream, barely enough to make it brown and not lose its sweetness. Not cocoa, not milk chocolate, mocha or hazelnut, just straight coffee, light black. Then I just sit back and I sip, sip, sip, sip, sip, and I sip, and then I say to you!

"Good morning my love"

I LOVE YOU MORE

I love you more, I love you more as your striking natural beauty begins to subtly wane and transform into your amazing character. I love you more when your clean scrubbed feminine aroma melds with the raptuousness of your voice and the mystique of your perfume of choice. I love you more.

I love you more, I love you more as elegance and sophistication gently replace the soft fragile features of your girlish face. I love you more, I love you more as your lips become slightly fuller and your hips gradually wider, and as your voice lowers just a fraction of an octave when you tell me how you love me. I Love you more.

I love you more, I love you more at those times when you're all flushed and aglow, like after love, or after giving birth, I love you more those times when you're wearing that hint of a smile of satisfaction, that's satisfaction for me and I love you more. I love you more for the way you see into my heart, choose for me that certain gift, provide me with that most timely lift, I love you more.

I love you much much more for how you fill me and complete me, how you satiate my being. But I love you most because of how you need me and how you love me more!

THE DAYZY

The dayzy is not just one of those pretty maids lined up in a row, she is the featured blossom, the lead flower in the floral show. The dayzy is infitestfully fresh and new, spontaneous like a spring morning's dew. The dayzy can sway with effortless ease to the natural flow of the evening breeze. She will not bow or bend down to the sun's warm rays until the lazy summer days end and only then does she rest, only then after having performed at her very best.

For she is the dayzy, an enchantress able to cloud up a man's clear masculine mind and make it hazy. Don't shower her with schemes or mystical dreams of grandeur, nor ordinary boudoir words of amour. No by chance fleeting romance, where loving is calculated and governed and touching and feeling and sensitivity is skance. No after all this is the dayzy, the feeling must make sense, the attraction must be mutual and the desire must be intense. Because the dayzy is my alternative to the rose, the ardor of her essence is sensuous to my nose. She can softly seduce a man like no other flower can.

"TO KNOW J.O."

To know J.O., you must walk with her slow, in the warm balmy sun, and in the biting wintry snow. To know J.O. you must dance with her slow to the love songs of the spinners, and not be beginners. But instant winners.

To know J.O., you must travel with her to the mystical places J.O. loves to go, like browsing around in quaint shops in little historic towns. You must dine on succulent and aphrodisiac quisine while sipping and savoring a tangy and fruity wine. Totally unconcerned with time.

To really know J.O., you must allow her to touch you close with her natural aromic confection, let her influence your direction, and in late spring as you both lie on a blanket in the grass face up to the sky peacefully, never even wonder why.

To know J.O., you first must know a sweet songstress with no wrongness in her songs, you must keep her safely in your memory where she belongs. I treasure the happiness that I shared with the J.O. whom I used to know, and the very best thing about the J.O. whom I used to know is that I take her with me everywhere I go.

A DARK SKINNED WOMAN'S LOVE

There is no love like a dark skinned women's love!

I'm talking about the opaque specimen of a worldly woman of color that I am completely in awe of. I mean a true dark skinned woman, seldom seen, not just medium brown but a black coffee ground brown Nubian queen is who I mean!

There is no touch like a dark skinned woman's touch!

No touch like her ebony touch, no other such touch can soothe a man half as much. No other hand can relax and comfort a man like her hand can. She has the warmest caress that any woman could ever possess. There is no other feeling like that feeling when she cradles you lovingly against her raison brown breasts, it is truly ecstasyesce.

There is no allure like a dark skinned women's allure!

The allure of her is affectuous and inffectious, her seduction is mysteriously demure, and it keeps a man coming back for more and more. Her scent is heaven sent, it is a sensuous blend of jasmine, marmalade, cocoa butter, and sage, the aroma of her lingers on and lingers on and never ever fades.

There is no kiss like a dark skinned woman's kiss!

It is a sweet tasting kiss like cane syrup, with a slight bite of ginger and a cinnemon twist. A dark skinned woman's kiss is the kiss I do not resist, it is my brown sugar, spicely nice, succulent and ambient to my lips like warm licorice ice.

From time eternal, a dark skinned woman has been the supreme queen of the headwrap, empress of the regal headdress, her sweet feet, ankles and toes have been bathed in fragrant oils and the essence of the rose. She has been wrapped resplendently in satin kinte, and silk, she is the mother of mankind, the spring of all mother's milk. No matter where she lays or plays, the essence of her always stays, a natural dancer and a male hormone enhanser, she is my personal answer.

Because there is absolutely no love like a dark skinned woman's love!

THE LADY FROM CAROLINA

The lady from Carolina is the quintessence of southern charm, regardless of her roots whether she is urban reared or rural farm, her disposition is always easygoing and warm. She is the fountain of my genetic seed and the inspirational visionary that I need to lead. She woos me and soothes me with amazing ease, and she comforts me gently like a cool Carolina breeze.

The lady from Carolina is a beauty of world renown. She stands proudly on her own among the most exquisite women around. She will never ever put on airs, but she has an infinate air about her which is truly rare. She is my sacred queen from her anointed feet to her haloed hair. Whenever I'm in need, the lady from Carolina is always there, ready to help, willing to share and anxious to show me how much she cares.

The lady from Carolina has talking eyes that she uses to look into your soul and tell you of her unconditional love, with no lies and no alibis. She has a stimulating presence and an intoxicating essence. She can fill out a designer dress or a high split skirt and look just as glamorous in blue jeans and a shirt. She is a stylist from the sun, she is my heroine, she is my chosen one.

The lady from Carolina will feed your body and give you food for your head. She will nourish your existence because that's how she's bred. She gives you your dessert first, like blackberry tarts baked with love straight from her heart. She'll give you spoonbread, creamy rice pudding and spiced meat, too sweet to eat. She serves you tea biscuits doused with marmalade and then she'll let you sip a tall cool glass of lemonade in the shade. And when it's all over the lady from Carolina will let you savor a snifter of her personal homemade plum wine, and it tastes sublime!

The lady from Carolina is inextricably wise. She is a bastion of feminine guile and guise. You won't often see her cry, no tears from those expressive eyes. Instead she'll juice you up real high and then slowly seduce you down with a kiss and a sigh. She is the original woman from the fold. My September rose, young middle aged or old, because in reality, she is my sister, she is my cousin, she is my aunt and my mother. She is my grandmother, my daughter, and my significant other. The lady from Carolina is very simply the epitome of grace, this phenominal woman from a Carolina place.

AFRICAN VANILLA CREME

I call her my African vanilla creme, although she's not always what she seems, still she is the answer to this ebony man's every dream because she possesses a natural kind of beauty not normally seen. She's just a bright negro girl with a strawberry blond curl and a skin tone exclusively her very own. African vanilla creme is not just some ordinary cuisine or color scheme, she's just a smooth and mellow frothy cream vanilla, what we call a bone a fair skinned colored girl just a skance past high yella.

African vanilla creme is my favorite flavor, she is the one confection that my palate savors. She is my personal sweetner, the tongue licking icing on my special birthday cake, and the light mocha toffee finger that stirs the morning coffee I take. African vanilla creme is the sauce that my soul needs, her sugar breath and pulsating caramel breasts are the delicacies on which I feed, she is the garden of my seed.

Visulize her ever changing hazel eyes, a mis-ethnical desquise which she utilizes with guise. Picture her wearing the free flowing open sunshine dress that I like best, or even in her tasteful state of complete undress, together we dance in our own certain way, just us and the wind, and nature accentuated by the light of the day.

SEX AT SUNRISE

I strongly subscribe to sex at sunrise, early at the dawning of a brand new day's first loveplay, while bathed in the morning sun's warm first ray is the ideal way to begin each day. Basking in the bliss of the day's first sunlit kiss.

Suppose in the morning before you arose, your first awakening scent was the ardor of a rose which your lover had lovingly placed in front of your nose and together you both lie, witnessing the darkness evolve to dawn and into a sunlit sky, you don't wonder why, you just know that it's no lie, it hides behind no disguise. It is each new dawning morning's sensual surprise, and that is why I fully ascribe to the manifestation of "Sex at Sunrise".

A COAL BLACK WOMAN

A coal black woman can light up any place. A coal black woman can glow like purple anthracite and illuminate the night. When her figurial ignites, the blue/black flame of her fame warms and radiates and a quiet grace surrounds her space. On a cold grey day, like a deep dark spirit she will emerge contrastible and almost thrice dimensional to smite the blues away. Brilliantly she looms, piercing gloom and conquering doom, a coal black woman brings hope and pride to a tired and weary race as all eyes focus attentively on her licorice face, everyone can see that truly a coal black woman can light up any place.

SISTERS, DO BROTHERS NOTICE?

Sisters, do the brothers notice all of the things you do to please them? When you do them, do the brothers really see them? Do they notice when you're wearing that special outfit or that stunning new dress, do they notice or do they just guess? Do they reciprocate when you put forth that radiant smile after they've been away for a long long while? Do brothers notice the brightness in your eyes when things are going well, when your not feeling well, can the brothers tell?

Sister, does the brother recognize the assurance in your voice whether you're talking to him face to face at home or from miles away by telephone? Does he see and smell the scented candles and fresh cut flowers which you place in his favorite space? Does the satisfaction show on his face? What about that special care put into that certain recipe, which you lovingly prepared? That chiffon pie or that coconut cake that you baked especially for his sake? Does he compliment you on your hair? Does he kiss you when you awake? When you dine out together does he pull out your chair?

Yes sister, brothers do notice things, they hear clearly how your heart sings, they can pick up quickly on the signs when you're in that loving state of mind. They have a knack for knowing when your romantic juices begin flowing, they can tell the difference when you want to be danced with and when you simply want to be held, and they know when you're ready to meld! Sisters, brothers always remember your particular kiss, hot like a searing cinnemon ember, they cannot easily forget, your particular kiss, so soft, so soulful, so wet. So sisters, to the question of whether brothers notice? I must confess, to some things peculiar to them, the answer is yes!

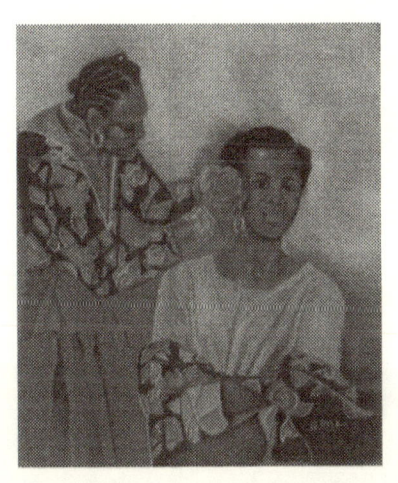

WHEN OTHERS WON'T LISTEN YOUR GRANDMOTHER STILL WILL

True self reliance and deep spiritual guidance, that's what our grandmother lovingly brings. Our grandmother is our maternal guardian angel right here on earth, we just can't see her wings. Our grandmother is our martyr, she is our family starter, our quality life liver and our personal care giver. Grandmother is our vintage kinage. She is the precious golden stream through which flows our proud family lineage.

So no matter what your secret delemma, whatever your private plight, call on your grandmother anytime, morning, daytime or night, with grandmother the time is always right. So if you're in trouble, if you're stressed, confused, alone or ill, always remember when others won't listen, your grandmother still will.

DARK WIDOWS

She is Rachael Robinson, the lady was Jackie's girl. She is the golden brown heroine who inspired him to challenge the world. She was his strength, his confidence, his shield, on and off the baseball field. Through stress and strife, together they redefined American life. With Jackie she knocked down baseball's "whites only" wall and she walked with him as he entered its "hallowed" hall. Her name is Rachael Robinson and she was Jackie Robinson's wife.

She is Myrlie, she was Medgar Ever's solid rock, she was the unshakable, source who enabled him to carry his personal cross. Medgar's devoted spouse, she was his soulmate, his confidante and the keeper of his house. She remained steadfast by his side, even to his death, Myrlie held strong, never abandoning her quest, never letting it rest, and when Medgar's murderer was convicted we all said yes...she is indeed, Myrlie Evers Williams, a dark widow at her best.

We called her sister Betty, she was Malcolm's apple brown mate. She was chosen to bear his children, destined to witness his fate. When minister Malcolm was purged, Dr. Betty Shabazz emerged a shining symbol of dignity and class. She was spirited and strong, she was sanquine and serene, she was Dr. Betty Shabazz, a dark widow supreme.

This lady is Coretta Scott, whom Martin chose as his queen. A more regal woman the world has rarely seen. She is a tower of character, power beauty and grace. Dignity and pride emanates from her face. Years after Martin's untimely demise, sister Coretta still continues to rise. Like a mother eagle Coretta soars, creating opportunities and opening doors. She spreads her wide wings and creates many wonderful things, she is the magnificent dark widow who wears Martin's ring.

Dark widows four, courageous mothers all. Powerful examples who answered the call. We cherish you, we love you, we honor your name. Our treasured American dark widows of fame.

GRAND DAMES

I am remembering now, the grand dames of my life. I am remembering those leading ladies who starred during my youth, and who mentored me and nurtured me in love and in truth. They were my first teachers, my first "live a clean life" preachers they were charmers, my personal heart warmers in hot combed hair with tight pressing oiled curls, encouragement givers to us small child boys and girls.

I am remembering all of those grand dames with the pleasant dispositions and the memorable names. As I now write and fondly reminisce, it seems that I can still taste my grandmothers chocolate cake and applepie kiss. It seems to long since I've seen my sweet Aunt Josephine, and I still recall the soul of aunt Mozelle and the independence of Aunt Rosabell. Nowhere were there any kinder than my Aunt Dee Dee, my aunt Thelma, and Aunt Adeline from Carolina, and also that gracious Sadie and her sister Clysie, who treated my sister and me extra nicely. I miss you aunt honey, I miss you too Millie, expressions of love and appreciation from me, little Billy.

I wish I could again see my mother and her best friend Lee, who along with Aunt Bert kept a close eye on me. If I could, I would bring back Wilhelmina, I would telephone Parthena, I'd say come back home Artelia, come and stay awhile Odelia. If I could I would sit again with pride in a church pew by Nannie's side and on a warm spring day, I'd take Aunt Lucy on an automobile ride.

To all of those grand dames, my message remains the same, even if I forgot for a minute your memorable name. I believe that I shall one day again see, all of the grand grand grand dames who meant to much to me.

I MISS YOU

I really miss you! I miss the actual you, the real you. I miss those flickering candlelit eyes you used to have which now seem so steely and hard. I miss the natural motion of you, I miss that sashay in your sway that you had as you moved along your way. The memories of you make me want to say, come back my fine fancy free, come home where you belong, both of us were wrong, return to me!

I really miss you! I miss you because life without one's wife is not always altogether freeing to a strong male being. Divorce is such a cold and unyielding force when it travels its usual unfeeling course. The emptyness it leaves is an undeniable loss, it seems to me that neither one of us ever even considered the extent of the hurt nor the emotional cost. You are the life partner whom I lost and truthfully, I miss you!

WHAT TALL GIRLS DO

What do tall girls do? Tall girls intimidate small guys, and they look tall guys straight in the eye. Tall girls can reach things from afar and from high upon shelves. They don't ask for any man's help, they just do it themselves. When dancing with a man who is prone to concede, tall girls seize the initiative and take the lead. Because inevitably tall girls are more unique than all girls in the ways that they compete.

For instance on the tennis court, tall girls usually win before they begin. Just like Althea, just like Martina, and just like Chrissy, Venus and Serena. What could be more striking than a tall girl filling out a fine tailored suit, in the courtroom looking lean and legal, or a long legged model in size eleven spiked heels, strutting not waddling in the new world fashion statements of today, flaunting her stuff while working the runway.

Have you seen a tall girl bellydance yet, or shine in a country line dance step? Can a tall girl perform nimbly on the parallel bars? Can she walk a highwire or fly a trapeze high among the stars? I don't know, but I would never say no, because there aren't many horizons left which a tall girl hasn't conquered yet!

I say keep growing tall girl, until you're ten feet tall.

AZURE

Azure! Azure! Of this I am sure,
Sweet tiny babe, your memory I
Shall always save. Your little
Voice I can still hear, your
Pretty little face I can still
See. I cherish the little time
You spent with me.

Azure! Azure! Of this I am very sure.